# FORGIVING THE GIRL INSIDE

# Forgiving the Girl Inside

## FINDING BALANCE, FREEDOM & FUN IN YOUR LIFE

## Lisa Drennon

Lisa A Drennon, Inc

# Contents

**Self-Published Author**
**Rochester NY**

**Editor: Debra Pavicic**

Book Layout © 2020 Business Growth Advisors

1st ed.
ISBN 9781736286708
Published 2020
Lisa Drennon

I dedicate this book to my Lord and Savior Jesus Christ. Because of HIM, I am. To my husband Kip who stood by my side through my emotional rollercoaster ride, thank you for your loyalty, commitment, and encouragement. To my children Joshua, Dehlia, and Dalton I'm honored to be your mom, thank you for teaching me all the things.

*When you are not sure what to say or pray, say "My Jesus, my Confidence."*

—Josephine Speranza

# About The Author

Child of God, wife, mother, grandmother, loyal friend, life coach, and avid reader. She loves the beach, mountains, and chocolate. She has worked full-time with a side gig for over thirty years. Her passion is to work with coaches and team leaders to help them surrender self-sabotage that keeps them stuck in fear so they can secure their soulmate clients, provide life-changing results, and 10x their income. Her dream is to open Divine Timing Ministries, an organization that will help women all over the world choose life for their unborn babies.

My mission for clients: In 12 weeks I help you surrender self-sabotage that keeps you stuck in fear so you can secure your soulmate clients, provide life-changing results, and 10x your income. In this unique coaching program, I help you release anger, frustration, & reliance on unhealthy coping mechanisms so you can live with balance, joy, freedom, fun, and deep forgiveness for past choices. This program works because we focus on changing thoughts and patterns, setting goals, and implementing a customized strategic plan to change habits that improve mind, body, and spirit, and gain control of the chaos and turn it into calm. Using a modality tailored to you, I share the keys to surrender self-sabotage, release fear, and implement healthy coping mechanisms so you can authentically and confidently provide life-changing results and create balance, freedom, and fun to catapult your success.

This unique modality is different from anything else you tried because it's tailored to you, no more one plan fits all. We begin with a personal assessment which is the framework we use to customize the plan for your specific needs. Everybody is different so each plan is uniquely tailored to fit your needs, to help you be balanced in the areas you need it most.

Are you tired of trying programs that are "guaranteed to get results" and within a week you go back to your old habits, or worse yet, you don't see a change? Here are three reasons why my program is different from all the other programs you've heard about.

#1: Transform effort into results, stay focused, and on track with daily accountability. Studies prove it is one of the key factors for success. By taking responsibility for the outcomes of your actions and decisions, you will be successful in your personal transformation. Within the first 3 weeks, you will see significant changes in your daily habits, feel your emotions become more stable, and enjoy a more balanced fitness.

#2: Implementing S.M.A.R.T. goals is the key to consistency. During the weekly coach calls, we review your personal goals and assure you are on track for success. Adding my secret sauce to your daily routine gives you the mindset to break bad habits and stay focused on the end result you desire. Whether your goal is to gain self-confidence, rewire your mindset to attract clients, increase energy levels, or balance emotions, consistently applying this key to your daily practices will get the results you desire.

#3: My custom-designed blueprint is tailored specifically to making it the perfect strategy to achieve the results you desire. Think of your fitness as a wheel. When it is out of balance, it doesn't roll very well. Focusing on key areas, we pinpoint where the wobble is and focus on the ones that need the most attention. This proven strategy has helped hundreds of life coaches improve and keep all areas balanced.

Results propel when we focus on accountability, consistency, and a strategic plan customized to your personal and professional life. Instead of wasting time on a yo-yo, one-size fit guide, get a strategic, customized plan tailored to your specific needs, and get the results you desire that will last a lifetime when implemented daily. Surrender self-sabotage, release fear and implement healthy coping mechanisms so you can authentically and confidently provide life-changing results and create balance, freedom, and fun to catapult success for both you and your client.

**Schedule your free 90-minute Blueprint Mastermind Strategy Session:**

**https://calendly.com/lisa-d-the-facets-coach/ 90min-mastermind-strategy-session**

**or   visit me at https://lisadrennon.com**

# Chapter One

## I Swore I Would Never Tell

A flash, a new memory, I heard the noise of suction, the doctor's voice say, "Relax this won't take long."

Sobbing uncontrollably, eyes swollen shut, snot dripping from my nose, I screamed "What have I done? No, no, no! I'll never be forgiven, never."

Then, I did it again. I do not recall how long it took me to make the same mistake twice. It does not matter, at least that is what I told myself. Darkness permeated my thoughts, sadness covered my heart, self-sabotage took over and my spoken words were like venom.

I was a murderer. Not once but twice. Confused, depressed, angry. I hated everyone, I hated myself. No one deserves forgiveness, especially me.

A hot mess emotionally, spiritually, and physically, I became bitter, spiteful, and disgusted. I thought of the lives that were never to be, reflected on the lies I chose to believe, and made weak attempts to justify these horrific acts. I convinced myself that it was my choice, my body, my right. Why did I get pregnant anyway? Wasn't God able to fix it? Why is sex wrong? Why would God allow a 16-year-old girl to get pregnant? Twice! I do not understand this God of religion and rules.

As I share this story I swore never to tell. I fight back tears and then allow them to freely flow. I have learned in my healing journey that tears are cleansing. It is our body's way of cleaning out the junk inside that keeps us trapped in lies, trapped in feelings of hurt, shame, and guilt. I have learned that releasing my tears allows me to embrace forgiveness and unbury the deep sadness in my heart.

For over three decades I tried to bury my shame and guilt, hiding behind unhealthy coping mechanisms of addiction, retail therapy, and overeating. By no means am I a slow learner. I felt I deserved perpetual punishment. My acts were horrific, and I deserved nothing but pain. My heart ached and anger seethed through my very being.

My healing journey continues. Each year I chip away at the brick wall built solidly around me. My heart experienced healing when I adopted the modality I share in this book. The first was having an attitude of gratitude, followed by taking back control of my emotions and finally learning to forgive yours truly. It has been a long journey, and it has taken perseverance to arrive at this wonderful, peaceful place of self-forgiveness, a place where I know in my heart that my Creator truly forgives me. A place where I know I can truly forgive others. A place filled with joy and freedom. "Seek and you shall find..." forgiveness is peace, forgiveness is joy, forgiveness pardons the offender and sets them free, even when yours truly is the transgressor.

EACH AND EVERY DAY IS A HAPPY NEW DAY. LEARN FROM YOUR PAST, GROW IN THE PRESENT, AND SOAR IN YOUR FUTURE.

—Drennon

**Forgiveness releases**

**the repressed**

**emotions**

**that cause the**

**bitterness**

**deep in our hearts.**

# Chapter Two

Becoming Aware

I stared blankly. My mind was numb. My feet were frozen. I couldn't move. I couldn't blink. I just stood there as my mother screamed in my face, her droplets of spit spraying my cheeks. She was always angry with me. Every weekend we would have the same fight. She would yell and scream about me being out until the wee hours of the morning doing my own thing. She would call me names, swear word names that I will not print here, but words that cut like a knife to my core. I believed all that she said about me.

I was no good. I was ugly on the inside. I was nasty and rude and hateful. I fought hot tears that desperately wanted to flow freely from my eyes that winced with every word. She continued to yell, words oozing that felt like knives cutting down my spine. It should have hurt. I should have fought back. But I just stood there. Listening to each venom-filled word spewing all over me, permeating my eardrums.

Looking back, I am surprised that I was such a coward. Fear paralyzed me. I cowered in a corner; it stole my voice. Jaw clenched tight. Mouth dry. Anger seethed. Stuff it down. Do not express yourself. Do not cry. Stay in control. DON'T let them see your weakness.

Such was the battle for more than 30 years. WOW! That is more than half my life. I was a hot mess and afraid to admit it or to show it. Boys do not cry, and neither should girls. After all, I was the youngest of three older brothers. Being the only girl, I had to be tough. No one was going to kick me around. No one was going to see this girl shed tears. Hell to the no. I got this. Or so I thought.

If only I had the tools back then that I have now. Life would have been so different. I may have saved a few relationships. I may have saved a lot of my own heartache. But nope, not in the plan. You see, I believed it was my punishment - that things had to be this way. I still believe everything happens for a reason and that all of this had a purpose. Whether it is to prune us or strengthen us, nothing is brought to us without a point. I learned some things through my experience. I learned that what appears to be the truth is not always the truth and white lies are real.

My biggest takeaway? Unforgiveness will destroy you.

Holding onto hurt, bitterness, shame, and guilt will eat you alive. Harboring anger consumes your thoughts, your time, and your being. Is it worth it? NO!

It took me years of therapy to understand that forgiveness has nothing to do with forgetting. It doesn't mean you release the debt or that the offense goes unpunished. It doesn't mean that you continue the same relationship you had prior to the offense. It doesn't mean you are obligated to appease the person.

So, what is forgiveness? Forgiveness is freedom. It is releasing the hurt with no commitment, no expectation, no nothing. Forgiveness is a choice - a decision to let go and be free from the person who committed the offense. Forgiveness is overcoming the negative with empathy. Forgiveness is peace. Forgiveness brings hope.

I often hear people say they refuse to forgive, or because they are not the offender, there is no need to forgive. This stinking thinking keeps us trapped in emotional pain that feels like a chokehold. Did you know that emotions are so powerful they affect our body? Studies[1] show that what we consider common pain is an indicator of a suppressed emotion:

- **Headaches and Migraines:** may indicate stress and tension
- **Neck Pain:** may indicate difficulty forgiving those you're bothered by
- **Shoulder Pain:** may indicate carrying a big, emotional problem; you're essentially "carrying the weight of a problem on your shoulders."

- **Upper-Back Pain:** may indicate you're feeling unloved or do not have enough emotional support
- **Lower-Back Pain:** may indicate money problems or lacking both emotional and financial support
- **Elbow Pain:** may indicate resistance to change in life

When I realized my body was in pain because my emotions were buried so deep, I knew I needed to change something: forgiveness was long overdue. Reflecting on the guilt and the shame of all the angry outbursts I have had, disgusts me to recollect them.

After I chose to terminate not one, but two pregnancies, depression rooted its bitter seeds deep into my heart. I cried hysterically for months, often burying my head in my pillow to stifle my uncontrollable screams. Every now and then my mom would ask if I wanted to talk. Of course not - not to her anyway. The last thing I wanted was a lecture saying I was damned to hell and I better stop fornicating. Self-sabotage had the upper hand, I had convinced myself that I was alone, no one would help, not even Jesus who my mom talked about ALL the time.

My mom Josie loved the Lord and his earthly mom, Mary so much, it's all she talked about. Growing up we had prayer cards, statues, and pictures of Jesus hanging on the wall. Everywhere you turned, you saw Jesus. Even on her death bed, she relied on him. I can still hear her loud and clear. I had just walked into her hospital room at Unity. It was a week before she passed. As I arrived, she lifted her head from her pillow and she said, "I'm going home."

I looked at her confused because she was deathly ill. "Mom, what do you mean? Home to Floren Drive?"

"No, home with Jesus, Mary, and Joseph. This is it." For as long as I could remember, my mom was ill with some chronic illness. Often my brothers and I would dismiss her ill-health. But this time, I knew her time on earth was coming to an end, and I was okay with that. Why? Because SHE was.

My mom probably didn't realize it but she left a beautiful legacy. Her love for Jesus was so strong, so incredibly powerful, I couldn't help but want to know Jesus myself. As far back as I could remember, age four perhaps, I asked all about Him and His Father God and wanting to read the Bible. My mom gave me children's books that illustrated beautiful stories such as Noah's Ark, the Ten Commandments, and the Easter Story. I was always looking for stuff to read, to learn and grow.

So in my search for a pen one day, it was no wonder I found the golden yellow prayer card titled: "The Abortion Tree."[2] It lay, on top of a hundred other prayer cards. I never asked if it was intentional. As far as I knew my mom was clueless about my abortions. I scanned it quickly and a whimper escaped my throat. I grabbed it and raced to my room, shutting the door behind me. As I sat on the floor, I just rocked and read, rocked and read, tears streaming down my face that turned into uncontrollable sobs. Clutching the card in my hands and saying the words over and over again brought no comfort. My cries turned into prayers. I remember my mom always telling me, "Lisa, if you don't know what to pray, just say My Jesus, my Confidence."

The more I prayed, the worse I felt. I could feel angst wrap itself around my heart, my mind, my spirit. *"Murderer! Filthy, no good, baby killer, scum. Jesus isn't going to comfort you."* I do not know where those whispers had come from, but they were loud. To this day, tears pour down my face, sobs escape my throat as I process this horrific state of mind. Lost. Alone. Devasted. Clueless as to what my future held. I cried out in terror. Fear seized me, *"NO! Please GOD forgive me, I am the WORST sinner of them all. I am so sorry. I don't know why or what, there is no reason, but I am sorry. Babies in heaven, please, please, please, forgive me. Are you in heaven? I was lied to. They told me you were blobs-with no life, oh my GOD what have I done?"*

Typing this, I see myself clear as day, rocking on the floor sitting with my legs under me, crying hysterically, "Lord, please, please forgive me. I promise I will NEVER abort again. Please, if I ever get pregnant again, I will carry my baby to full term and raise him to honor and glorify YOU. I will teach him Your ways. Please don't punish the child. Let my babies be healthy, please..."

*Yes, you had me murdered before I was born.*
*Yet I might have been the one*
  *The only one to care for you*
  *To soothe and comfort you, my Mom.*
 *No one can predict the future.*
*Who knows what your sufferings may be*
  *I won't be around to help you Mom*
  *You hung me on the Abortion Tree.*

The poem is signed M.F.D.


Bringing this hurt up, reflecting on this buried moment baffles me. Did I really not learn my lesson? Why was I so naïve, so desperate for love? Was I really going to go out and get pregnant again? Yep!

In August of 1985, I became pregnant again. This time I was ready. At 17 years old, I stood tall and proud. The moment I knew, I told my mom, and in May of 1986, I gave birth to a beautiful son, who by the way, is an amazing man, an incredible husband, and the best father. I should have realized I was forgiven when I met my husband Kip and GOD blessed us again with two beautiful children, both also amazing in every way. I should have realized GOD forgave me as I watched my children grow into amazing adults with hearts of gold and incredible health, strength, and loving hearts. But nope, I chose to believe that forgiveness was not for me. Instead, I lived with self-sabotage.

How blind I was. Blind to a fault, I couldn't see my blessings. I am not sure when self-sabotage set in, well before my teens. Even as a teen mom, I struggled with my ability to be patient and kind. It was like nervousness was hereditary. I was so easily aggravated. Years later I realized that the abortions affected my emotional health. I was on an emotional rollercoaster ride combined with unhealthy coping mechanisms that impacted my relationships, my ability to cope with simple things. I didn't even know how to recognize my feelings. Everything came out in anger.

I remember the time when I was interrupted on a trip to Canada. I had to stop my adult conversation to take my then 18-month-old son to the bathroom. I had a full-blown temper tantrum, aggravated that I had to be interrupted. Why? Because I was incredibly anxious. But instead of realizing that, I would just scream at the top of my lungs (which triggered an asthma attack) to let go of my frustration. I always wondered what was wrong with me. I always felt pretty messed up.

It baffled me to realize that I didn't even know how to identify feelings until my 40s. What was anger, fear, frustration, sadness? For me, it didn't matter. It all came out in a rage, full-blown screaming and yelling fits of fury rage. I wish I would have had post-abortion care. If I only knew back in my 20s what I learned in my 40s, my relationships wouldn't have been such a hot mess.

But being the typical, stuff-and-explode, red/green, extroverted personality type, I blamed my parents, my poverty - everyone but me. I was a victim! Looking back, I was miserable. As a single teen mom, I had no choice (or so I was told) but to live at home with a controlling mother who didn't trust that someone like me could be a good mom. I was such a horrible person and was reminded of it daily. I lived in hell and wanted out.

Often, I would snap for no reason, or what I learned later, appeared to be for no reason. My deep hurt and stuffed emotions wanted out so they came out side-ways - in anger. After Kip and I married, there were several times I would snap at him for no apparent cause. One of my therapy sessions dug up the reason - the repressed emotions of shame and guilt kept me in that state. Never feeling like I was good enough, not a good wife, good housekeeper, etc., I would spin my wheels trying harder only to feel defeated and even more of a mess-up.

You see, memories of my horrific choices stirred up negative feelings of worry, fear, and abandonment. Trust was not a word in my vocabulary nor was respect or healthy boundaries. It went deeper than the teen years. It stemmed back to the age of six or seven. When I was in second grade, my mom had a nervous breakdown. Her father had just died. She sobbed uncontrollably, tearing at his crumpled-up picture held tightly in her fist. The ambulance came and took her, putting her in a straitjacket. My older brother told me I had to go to school, but I did not want to - mommy wasn't right. I remember thinking to myself, "*I don't ever want to be like that.*"

But I was. I was aware of my triggers and completely ignored them. Why? I was clueless about how to prevent it. So, from an incredibly young age until my mid-thirties, I let shame, guilt, and anger control my every thought. Explosive anger was my M.O.

What I learned and observed when I was little, I now know I can unlearn. I can implement a new strategy, a healthy modality that digs deep into the bitter roots and breaks free from the twisted lies. The first thing I realized? My anger infiltrated daily conversations.

I became aware of my triggers: a tingling on the back of my neck, rapid breathing, racing heart, and knots in my stomach. I realized that if somebody said something, I would ponder their statement, and rather than confront them and say "Hey, what you just told me was very hurtful," I would say nothing. I would let it steep and instead, have sideways anger and strike whoever was in my path. TMJ, back, neck, and migraines became the norm. When I started listening to my body, I decided to make a change. I began researching every book on anger. I met with a counselor and began therapy.

Throughout the years I did all sorts of things. Some things helped; some didn't have any impact at all. Nothing helped me manage my outbursts. My emotions were a roller coaster ride and I desperately wanted off. My therapy sessions were intense, yet all I came away with was to count to 10 and speak in "I" statements. Okay, well that band-aid did not stick. When I realized I needed to dig the root up, that's when the change began.

When I became aware that my stinking thinking kept me stuck, that it dictated my body language, that certain phrases triggered me, I finally understood how to take the first step - how to forgive, to let go, to be heard. God handed me the tools a long time ago, but I was too busy hiding behind shame and guilt, too afraid to look fear in the eye, too proud to accept the gift. What I learned when I held that first tool in my hand was the beginning of a beautiful journey - a healing journey that transformed a lot of lives.

There's a lot of misconception about forgiveness. Many believe that in order to forgive, you have to forget. That is the furthest from the true meaning of forgiveness.

Forgiveness is not reconciliation. It is not forgetting. It does not condone the act nor excuse the person who did it. Forgiveness does not erase the consequence, it does not do away with justice, it rises above it.

Forgiveness is a decision. It is a choice to let go. If you choose not to forgive, you might carry a deep bitterness and anger. This may affect other relationships and experiences you may have. This bitter root may cause depression or anxiety. It may even keep you trapped inside your head listening to the negative voices.

When you choose forgiveness, you choose freedom. You release your anger, your hatred, and your revenge. This does not mean you are reconciling with your offender - oh no, it's the complete opposite.

You see, it takes ONE person to forgive. It takes two to be reunited. When you make a decision to forgive, the other person doesn't even have to know. They probably don't even care, or they are clueless that there is a problem. Forgiveness is NEVER dependent upon the other person asking you for forgiveness.

Forgiveness happens inside the wounded person. Reconciliation happens in a relationship. Ideally, when someone has hurt you, you may want to restore the relationship. The offender may be a close friend or relative. The offense most likely damaged the bridge of trust. When you choose to forgive, you are not giving that person permission to reconcile, you are simply setting yourself free from the offense.

We can forgive a person who never says they're sorry. We cannot truly reconcile unless that person honestly is sorry. We can forgive even if we do not trust the person who wronged us. Reconciliation can happen only if we decide to trust the person again. That trust has to be earned.

Forgiving someone has no strings attached. Reconciliation comes with conditions. Forgiveness does not mean you are a doormat. It doesn't mean you are allowing that person to hurt you again. Forgiveness is not a license for an offender to keep repeating their action because they know you will forgive them.

Forgiveness is for all people. We forgive because God forgives us. God's forgiveness is for all people, but not all people are reconciled to God. Forgiveness is freedom, freedom from the chokehold it keeps us in when we decide not to forgive. Forgiveness releases the repressed emotions that cause the bitterness deep in our heart. Forgiveness brings peace and empathy. It sets you free.

It wasn't until I understood forgiveness that I realized I needed to forgive. I had no problem extending that to everyone else but myself! No, I did not deserve it. Besides, how can you possibly reconcile with yourself? This negative thinking kept me stuck for thirty years! Instead of seeing myself through my Creator's eyes, I saw myself as a filthy rag, an old rotten cloth to be tossed aside the way I tossed aside two precious lives. Nope, I decided repeatedly that I was undeserving but well deserving of the self-sabotage and punishment I continuously doled out to myself each and every day.

# Forgiving the Girl Inside

A Healing Journey from Shame &
Guilt to
Loving Yours Truly Unconditionally

**A**wareness   of

**W**hat  your

**A**natomy

**R**eveals  in  your

**E** motions

Forgiveness releases

the repressed

emotions

that cause the

bitterness

deep in our hearts.

# Chapter Three

## A DIFFERENT PERSPECTIVE

When my kids were growing up, we stressed the importance of giving thanks, teaching them that stinking thinking created a rebellious attitude, and it was more important to be nice than it was nice to be important. We hung a *Gratitude* poster on the fridge as a reminder to be thankful. Countless times I walked by it and dismissed it. Little did I know that an attitude of gratitude would be my first pivot to my healing journey.

When we focus on the positive, we change our thoughts. It's a game-changer. Even now, when stinking thinking creeps in my thoughts, I quickly change it to positive comments. I try not to look back, but I always wonder why I knew this all along but was unable to implement it until I came across a book by Ann Volscamp, *One Thousand Gifts: A Dare to Live Fully Right Where You Are.* If you know me, you know that I love a challenge. Intrigued by a challenge from her book to write down 10 things you are grateful for each day until you reach 1000, I began to journal daily. It helped me so much, I surpassed the 1000 gifts, and to this day, I still write down 10 things I am grateful for.

I learned several things about myself during this time. I was stuck in my own way. The walls I built around me created a prison and trapped my pain. I couldn't see beyond the thick walls; all I saw was misery and despair. Focused on what could go wrong, did go wrong. I said I was ugly, and my self-esteem plummeted. I said I was overweight, and my waistline blew up. All the negativity recycled in a never-ending circle of regret.

To my surprise, when I focused on giving thanks, the bitterness inside me slowly faded. It no longer served me. Even now, when it tries to steal my joy, I immediately turn it around, changing the negative into positive. I am not overweight; I am healthy and thriving. I am not ugly; I am beautiful and created by God for greatness and a purpose.

My heart soared, and my thoughts were blissful. When my eyes open and before my feet hit the floor each morning, I thank the Lord for His breath of life and recite all the things I'm grateful for, especially another opportunity to serve heart-to-heart, to do His will, and focus on His purpose. This daily practice has totally propelled me to focus on others, to focus on being unselfish, and truly see people for who they are. My brick walls that were solidly built for three decades were starting to crumble. For the first time, I studied forgiveness and realized what it truly meant. It was a blessing to utter the words "I forgive you mom, dad, brother, sister, friend." Whoever needed forgiveness, I easily and freely extended it.

To finally break the myth buster of forgiveness was such a relief, (myth buster: forgiveness does not mean you forget) like a heavy wet blanket being removed. My load felt so much lighter all because I practiced an attitude of gratitude. When I chose to forgive, I asked the Lord to change my heart, to help me see my offender the way He does. More walls crumbled.

The emotional rollercoaster ride came to a halt. Anger, frustration, and bitterness visited less, and when they did come to visit, they did not stay long. Nervousness was knocked out along with the solid brick walls that kept me in darkness. When I realized giving thanks opened my heart and allowed me to forgive, my heart filled with joy. The best part? I did not expect anything in return from my offenders. It did not matter if they heard the words, "I forgive you" or not.

One of the lessons I learned: forgiveness is a choice. The offender does not need to ask for it nor do I need to say it face-to-face. I realized that forgiveness sets me free. I broke another myth buster: when you forgive, the relationship is restored, and you give full access to your offender - a lie to be squashed. When you realize forgiveness is a choice and you do not forget, nor do you let the person back in, that's when you can move forward. Being grateful for the lesson learned in the hurt that arose from the betrayal is healing.

Forgiveness is a healing that sets you free. It has nothing to do with the other person. It has to do with you choosing to forgive the way God forgives you. There are many keys to forgiveness, the one that set me free was having an attitude of gratitude. It is impossible to hold onto bitterness and unforgiveness when you are practicing a daily attitude of gratitude.

Ready to begin your healing journey? Each day grab a pen and paper, write down ten things you are thankful for: the birds flying in the air, flowers blooming in spring, a sink full of dirty dishes because it means you have a family to care for, a fridge full of food, a pile of dirty laundry, reliable transportation, your ability to see, taste, smell, hear, your beautiful child skipping on the sidewalk... you get the idea. Give thanks for all things and understand why you appreciate these special gifts, then feel your heart soar as you surround yourself with these beautiful treasures. I read once that if you woke up with only what you gave thanks for from the day before, what would you wake up with? It gets you thinking, doesn't it? Giving thanks in writing, gives you a new perspective, a different perspective. I have journals filled with what I am grateful for and why I appreciate these gifts.

I remember giving thanks for snow. A complainer at heart, I loathed bundling up and fighting the wind and snow. At the beginning of my 1000 gifts challenge, as I thought about things to write, I remembered that cold wintry morning. I awoke and did my morning things, bundled myself up, and leashed up my dogs, Tucker and Indi, for their morning walk. Dreading the cold wind and the heavy snowfall from the night before, I stepped outside to a blanket of snow-white beauty. The sidewalks hadn't been plowed. The snow was too high on the sidewalk, so I led the pups to the street. Walking down the middle of the road was magical. The streetlights reflected on the layers of light snow, glistening like diamonds, a beautiful memory to treasure. If an attitude of gratitude can change this beach girl's perspective on snow, well, it's time for you to grab your pen and notepad. I challenge you to begin your gratitude journal today.

**Forgiveness is healing that sets you free.**

# Chapter Four

**A ONE-WORD JOURNEY**

Focus. I had to laugh when I spoke to my coach about what to write for this chapter. I said to him, "How am I going to write a whole chapter on one word, what will I focus on?"

\*\*\*\*\*\*\*\*\*\*\*\*\*\*\*\*\*\*\*\*\*\*\*\*\*\*\*\*\*\*\*\*\*\*\*\*\*\*\*\*\*\*\*\*

My mind raced. My thoughts were all tangled like a bowl of spaghetti. That pretty much summed it up - chaos and out of control. Depression turned outward, the rage and disgust I felt ruled my mind. My emotions would fluctuate. I was on an emotional rollercoaster. I quickly would run and hide to cry my eyes out. Sadness permeated my entire being only to accelerate to frustration, escalate to screaming, yelling, and then silence. I stuffed my hurt, burying it deep inside my heart, behind brick walls that I could not see over.

Trapped, addicted to retail therapy, wine, and baked goods, I swore to myself I had it all under control. Instead, I was hiding behind unhealthy coping mechanisms that kept me unbalanced and overwhelmed. I was at my wit's end. Not wanting anyone to see me cry, I locked myself in the bathroom or took off in the car to escape my pain. With all the years I spent in therapy, you think I would be over this by now. Frustrated with being told to read one more book on anger, I stopped weekly visits only to realize I could not do this on my own.

It took a while to find just the right counselor. Like a good pair of jeans, you must keep trying until you get a good fit. As I walked into the office, I immediately knew this was a good fit. During the screening process, I was asked, "Lisa, if you could focus on one word, if you could change one thing, what would it be? What is one word you could focus on that will help you heal?"

My thoughts came to a sudden halt. Say what? In all my years of counseling, no one has ever asked me that before. Focus on me? Really? Okay, what is one thing I would like to see happen?

I replied, "Peace. I want peace. I am tired of being on an emotional rollercoaster ride, I am tired of yelling, screaming, and stuffing... I am tired. I want peace."

I did not fully understand how focusing on one word would help me. I was surprised to find that it was a major pivot in my healing journey. Not only was I able to find balance, but I also accomplished so much more than anticipated - a win for a multitasker like myself. Searching scripture for peace and praying that my life would be filled with it, I realized that my worry of a million things kept my emotions in chaos.

When I focused on all the things: taking care of my family, working full time, household chores, cooking, errands, appointments, practice, etc., I felt buried. Frustration and anger crept into my mind and overtook my thoughts. My one-word journey brought order to my life. I realized I had turned to many addictions to stuff my hurt. Baking was such an outlet, not a bad thing until you turn it into comfort food. Overstuffing my ever-increasing waistline kept my emotions unbalanced. I had no idea that refined sugar increased inflammation and played havoc on my fitness. Instead of bringing me joy, it increased my sadness. One of the many outlets that failed me, I did not understand how my actions kept me stuck. Slowly it was revealed to me. The more I concentrated on my one word, the further my progress. When confronted with a negative attitude, I was able to quickly respond with kindness instead of snarkiness. My family noticed the change and so did I.

What did I learn? To my delight, when I combined the one word with the gratitude journal, my heart began to change. Peace permeated my thoughts. Compliments sprung from my mouth and like ocean waves crashing on the shore, I felt peace for the very first time. I realized that peace brings forgiveness and forgiveness brings freedom.

Ultimately, isn't this what we are all looking for? Freedom? I realize that I was stuck on the emotional roller coaster and was in desperate need of "tunnel vision," a concept I have shared for years with my trainees and apply to my clients to this day. It really helps you focus on one thing. (Check out lisadrennon.com to order your "tunnel vision" merchandise).

We have so much come at us, in all directions from all sources. If you are red/green on the color personality wheel like me, you want to do all the things - research slows you down a bit but it really helps you to stay focused. So, what did I need to focus on? What did I really want?

This daily exercise was a major part of my healing journey. Each December I choose a new word. At first, it took a few days for me to get, now it comes before I even think about it.

Ready to choose your one word, to begin your healing journey? To select your one word, reflect on what you desire the most. What is one area in your life you want to see improve?

~What are your goals?

~Where do you need transformation?

~How do you want to make changes in your personal life? Your professional life?

Pray for that one word to be revealed to you. Once you have it, write it down. Make a poster, put a reminder on your phone, research it. Look up its definition, find the root, the original language. Search Scripture for it, dig deep into what it truly means.

This one word will be your focus for an entire year. It's common to study it from January to December but your year can be whenever you want. I always say there's no time like the present for a change. Don't wait until January to begin this journey, choose it now and watch how the one-word focus changes your heart, actions, and your mindset.

# Peace brings forgiveness, forgiveness brings freedom

# Chapter Five

**REGAINING CONTROL**

I don't recall the exact moment I regained control. I do remember the look on my mother's face when I stood up for myself. For whatever reason she didn't think I was capable of being an adult, so she constantly interfered with my decisions. The more independent I became, the more she tried to gain control. In her eyes, I did nothing right and she often did things without my consent. Even after I was married, I felt like I didn't do anything right. Maybe it was because I became a mom at 18 or perhaps the lack of self-esteem I carried.

I like to think my immaturity kept me stuck, but like anyone else, I wanted to play the blame game. I guess nerves and unbalanced hormones played a part or maybe the shame and guilt I buried so deep in my heart made me a coward. Whatever the reason, I wasn't strong enough to maintain healthy boundaries. It was easier to be controlled than it was to stick up for myself. Boundaries were crossed and I was constantly ordered around by the adults in my life. When I fought back, things were thrown up in my face. Threats and reminders of how much was being done for me, how ungrateful I was, and how selfish I had become were all words that stung and were used as weapons to keep me under their control.

Fear was my driving force. Instead of moving towards freedom, I dove into the bondage of addictions. Those would be my escape. Alcohol numbed the pain and smoking prevented panic attacks. Unhealthy on so many levels, I was exhausted and wanted off the emotional rollercoaster. Paralyzed with worry, I stayed put. It was as if my feet were cemented to this life of misery. I deserved all the punishment and torture I received. After all, I was a monster, a murderer. Why should I live a joy-filled life? I deserved to lose my power, I deserved perpetual punishment.

This insanity had to stop. Something in me snapped. Desperate to regain control, I sought counseling. This is where I learned "I" statements and how to establish healthy boundaries. With guidance from my counselor, I devised a plan and acquired the tools to regain control.

**Step one**: design a blueprint of my goals and dreams, my ticket to freedom. After all, I wasn't going to have other adults dictate my choices forever.

**Step two**: establish healthy boundaries. It was imperative to communicate my desires and take back control. I needed to be strong for mine and my family's sake. This was the most challenging, as it involved change and most people are resistant to change. I learned that consistency was key. I realized I needed to speak up and voice my concern when necessary. I also became aware of when to keep my opinion to myself as not every conversation needs a comment.

Reclaiming my power through this process taught me a few things. I learned that I am the only one who controls my feelings and my thoughts, no one else. Eye-opener: I **cannot control what other people** do or say, only how I respond. The power was mine when I maintained healthy boundaries. When others made demands on me and I silently obeyed, I lost my power. Silence is a strong voice. Saying nothing is automatic permission to give away control. To quickly gain it back, I used "I" statements, apologized for the confusion, and reiterated my position.

I also learned that mutual consent is a process that allows all parties to have their say. Making joint decisions instead of demands breeds respect and love. When confronted with a situation, it is helpful to ask the following:

> *How does this situation affect those involved?*
> *Do I need to consult with them?*
> *What do I want from them?*
> *Do I want their opinion?*
> *Is a joint decision necessary?*

A collaborative effort makes everyone feel important and assures boundaries will be maintained. Old patterns often sneak up. Consistent daily reminders prove helpful in maintaining my power.

I realized that part of my problem was holding on to hurts - past, present, and future. You know, the ones that run through our head when we don't trust someone and conjure in our mind how they will hurt us because of this, this, and that. Yeah. Stinking thinking caused my mind to be in a whirlwind. Of course, I'm one of those people who wear their feelings on their sleeve - no filter for this girl.

I had an understanding. I don't like women, didn't trust women, and no way was I going to nurture close relationships with women. In my senior year of high school, my best friend since the 7th grade betrayed me. I told her EVERYTHING. We were so close and thought we would be besties forever until the day she betrayed me. I will never forget that day. Yes I forgive her, no our relationship was never reconciled. Off we went our separate ways. A betrayal is difficult to reconcile. Forgiveness is easy, trust on the other hand must be earned My motto was sealed: TRUST NO ONE, especially women!

Horrible advice. Trust is a big part of forgiveness which is the major player in releasing depression. When we hold onto a hurt it causes depression turned inward, protruding outward to anger. When we stuff it, it can't stay there too long. It manifests itself sideways, affecting our sleep, nutrition, energy. It is truly emotionally draining. For me, my unprocessed thoughts crossed boundaries forcing me to entertain negative outbursts or worse, doling out the silent treatment. Refusing to forgive, even though I fully understood how easy it was, I chose to bask in my hurt.

As simple as it seems, choosing to say the words "I forgive you" isn't always so easy. Between our negative thought patterns, stories that we were told about holding onto our hurts, and the influence of others heck, society makes it hard. You see, forgiveness doesn't mean you trust the person, it just means that you release them for their offense, and you do not trust them but come to the understanding that what they did will not hurt you anymore. When you make a conscientious decision to forgive, you are simply saying, "I forgive you for hurting me." Period. That's it. Nothing else. Just say those six words. End of conversation. There's no "I'm sorry for (insert offense) but when you (start blaming), it made me (insert reason), etc." Don't get trapped in this false sense of forgiveness.

Forgiveness is a decision, not a feeling. It does not excuse the offender or minimize his or her offense towards you. Forgiveness is your decision to cancel debt another person rightfully owes you. Forgiveness is the intentional and voluntary process in which a victim undergoes a change in feelings and attitudes regarding an offense and lets go of vengefulness.

Forgiveness is a choice. It is an obedient response to God. It is personal and costs absolutely nothing. In fact, forgiveness equals freedom. It is an act of grace, mercy, and love. It is God's way of helping us come to terms with a world where people are often unfair to one another and hurt each other deeply. Forgiveness is liberating. It breaks the chains and allows you to be free to breathe.

Do you want freedom or bondage?
Depression or joy?
Anxiety or peace?

Choose forgiveness.

Remember, when you forgive it does not mean you are pretending nor forgetting the act never happened. It doesn't mean you are condoning the act or excusing the person who did it. It doesn't erase the consequences nor does it mean you invite the person in to hurt you again.

No, forgiveness is not reconciliation nor is it a feeling. It is not dependent upon the other person asking you for forgiveness. Forgiveness is an act of obedience to God – it is not an event, it's a journey.

Won't you take the first step?

Forgiveness
is a choice. It is an
obedient response
to God, it is
personal, and
it costs
absolutely nothing

# Chapter Six

**VICTOR NOT VICTIM**

When I first stepped out of the victim role, I was shocked at how my thought process changed. Before, I would readily jump into the victim mode, bash the person I was arguing with, and then cry for weeks or stew in my anger blaming that person for what a jerk he or she truly was. I hate to admit that I played the victim role way too long, mostly because I was clueless on how to exchange it for the victor crown. Of course, I began to read every book I could find on how to get along with others and finally enrolled in a course with Leslie Vernick, a Christian Author/Counselor. The transition restored my full power and by instilling her foundation teaching of CORE I took full responsibility for my own actions.

I realized that my inner strength, my confidence, and my commitment to take care of myself, was always accompanied by an "I" statement. See, when you have an "I" statement no one can take that away from you. Nobody can take away how you feel or how you react. Oftentimes we take the victim stance because we believe, whether right or wrong, that we are a victim. It happened to me and I thought I had no control over the situation.

This thought process was learned behavior, and whatever is learned can be unlearned. A victim has a choice. When we are hurting, we can choose to bury it deep inside our hearts or we can choose to accept it and process it. Oftentimes, we choose to bury it and then it will come out "sideways." Usually, when we see that person or hear they will be at the same gathering, the bitterness in our heart stirs up ugly thoughts and our blood starts to boil. To be free of this bitterness root, we need to dig it up. We need to acknowledge and accept the hurt and forgive the parties involved. Begin with yours truly. Yes, it is imperative that you forgive yourself. Forgive yourself for your part, for words you said or did not say, then forgive the offender. Refusing to forgive not only allows the root of bitterness to grow deeper, but it also plays havoc on your emotions which ultimately affects your overall health. If you are having trouble sleeping or you are turning to unhealthy coping mechanisms to cover up your pain, then you totally get what I am saying here.

I have worked with several women who felt like victims, especially with their moms and husbands. They fell to victimhood and were exhausted because they tried everything to stop the vicious cycle; the more they tried, the worse the relationship became.

Being a victim is lethal; the silent rage steals your trust and confidence, and makes you feel anxious and depressed. I will never understand why hurt people hurt others. I do know that to step out of the emotional rollercoaster, you need to stick up for yourself. You need to unlearn the victim role and master the victor stance. How? I am glad you asked. It takes a commitment on your part but can be easily mastered with three easy steps: Speak up, take responsibility for your own actions, and show compassion and understanding. I know, I know, you are tired of always being the one to make things better. I totally get that. But this is different. This time you are not trying to control the situation nor the person, you are simply changing your behavior.

***Speak up.*** Be aware of your triggers. We all know when our tone is going to come out snarky. Instead of letting anger control your response, respond in a loving way. If your mom is at your house and makes a derogatory remark about your house being dirty, simply reply, "Thank you so much mom for pointing that out. Things have been crazy here so I decided that cleaning day would be postponed until next week."

If you just spent three hours getting ready, picking out the perfect outfit and your husband says, "I hate that dress," simply reply, "Oh, I understand you don't like this dress, but I love how it feels." This does take practice but realize, it is well worth it, and when you respond in this way, you will acquire the victor crown.

**Take responsibility for your own actions**. This is a

bit more challenging, but hey, who does not like a challenge. Am I right? Open communication is the key. If you are on the brink of an argument, realize the offender is most likely not mad at you, you are simply a scapegoat. When the conversation escalates, do not engage. Simply reply that you do not appreciate their abusive language and you will continue the conversation when they have calmed down. Then walk away. Do not engage, do not say anything else. Go off by yourself, journal, pray, call your counselor, a trusted friend, go for a walk - just get out of the conversation and take a cool-down period. When you reconvene, if the person is not ready to talk, make an agreement to come back to the table to discuss the disagreement. Sometimes a person might never be ready, and that has nothing to do with you. Take it from me, you can only protect yourself, you can only change your actions.

When we own our part and take responsibility for our own actions, it changes the outcome of the conversation. I have avoided many arguments by practicing this. The first thing you want to do is ask yourself, "Does this situation have anything to do with me? Does it affect me directly?" The last thing you want to do is get involved in someone else's argument, Third parties need to stay out. If someone comes to you for advice, you need to cautiously proceed, and be sure that the person is making their own decision, coming up with their own conclusion. I have seen way too many people fall into victim mode after giving advice that the person acts upon, only to have it end badly, and guess who gets blamed? Yes, you. Be incredibly careful. My advice – don't give advice!

**The final step** *is to show compassion and understanding.* This was by far the most difficult for me because I am not an empathetic person. Sometimes I just shake my head when I observe conversations or when I am attacked by someone who is using me as their scapegoat. My instinct is to engage with negativity. Don't get sucked in! Therefore, it is so important to be aware of your feelings. Stay out of the victim mode by practicing compassion and understanding. When someone verbally attacks you, respond, "Oh, I'm sorry to hear you are upset, how can I help?" This immediately changes the offender's response because one, they were expecting a fight and two, they must stop and think why they were upset. Remember to keep your stance, maintain healthy boundaries, remember your "I" statements. Acknowledging their hurt opens the door to communicate effectively and keeps you from falling into the victim mode. Remember, you want to remain the victor regardless of what comes your way.

Are you ready to trade your victim hat for the victor crown? When you realize what your true purpose is, you understand that victimhood has no room. A victim cannot help others nor thrive. A victim does not live joy-filled nor have the desire to be successful. They have no power. That is not how you were created. You were designed by God for greatness and a divine purpose to do His work. You certainly cannot do it if you're spending time as a victim.

Being a victor sets you free. Acknowledge the hurt, process it, then release it. It is all part of the healing journey of deep forgiveness. Speak up, take responsibility, and show compassion and understanding. Be the victor you are meant to be.

Refusing to forgive not only allows the root of bitterness to grow deeper, but it also plays havoc on your emotions which ultimately affects your overall health

# Chapter Seven

**Brain Dump**

I am a visual learner. When I first learned to do a brain dump, I pictured my brain being poured out of my head like a bowlful of wrinkly worms dropping on a plate. Weird, I know. I desperately wanted to be rid of the negativity occupying my brain space. It was causing havoc on the rest of me. From overeating, drinking too much, and not sleeping enough, this sideways effect had to go. You know what they say? Anger is depression turned outward. Say what?! Boy, was I expressing a lot of anger!

I remember the very first time I did a brain dump. I was scared. First I thought, "There is no way I can write for 15 minutes. Did I even have that many thoughts?" I reluctantly set my timer and hesitated, panicked. I didn't really know what to write. Think, think, think! I was instructed to write whatever came to mind. Okay, I've got this. I wrote and wrote. Soon the timer went off and I couldn't believe I had written 20 pages. My next step was NOT to read it. Just let it be, pray over it. The next day I was to go back and circle common words, repetitive words. Then I was instructed to categorize them into columns titled: "Relationships, Career, Activities, Fun, and Faith" and any other categories that shared a common theme. WOW!

This brain dump brought up the painful memories of my horrific choices. As instructed, the day after, I set my timer again for 15 minutes. I organized my random thoughts into categories and was shocked at what I saw:

*I was holding so much anger towards family members, past choices, and the shame I carried deep within my heart. I made some horrific choices at the age of 16 - sweet it was not. I chose to have my first abortion. An unplanned pregnancy devastated my immature mind. I was in such a bad place, a dark place. I couldn't talk about it. I couldn't even express it. I did not even want to share it. I was so ashamed. I felt like scum.*

*Looking back at that decision, I was told abortion was no big deal. It was like a growth on your body, a bad tumor or a cyst. Thinking of it that way, it did not seem like a bad decision. This brain dump brought up the memory of walking into Planned Parenthood high on valium and whatever else. I recalled the pro-life protesters standing nearby with signs. A man held a sign that said, "Choose Life." He looked at me and said, "You don't have to do this. There is support for you." I stared at him blankly as I was*

*quickly pulled into the building. When I awoke hours later, I real-*
*ized I was away from that awful place but completely confused as to*
*where. My eyes were heavy. Struggling to open them, I noticed how*
*parched my mouth felt. I have never felt so drained, weak. My arms*
*were like lead. Scared, I felt like a child cowering in the corner,*
*not sure what to do. I heard a noise, a voice, it was garbled. I could*
*barely make out the words but then I felt it, a hard object being*
*pushed against my lips. The warm water hit my lips and relieved*
*the dryness. I gagged as I gulped it down. Then the voice asked*
*if I was hungry. Hungry? My stomach groaned. A burger smoth-*
*ered in ketchup was placed next to me on the bed. I realized how*
*starved I was and scarfed it down. It tasted like cardboard. I set the*
*plate down and observed the pile of ketchup smeared on the white*
*plate and that's when I saw it, horrified, I gasped. The white sheets I*
*sat upon were covered, my legs-covered, blood smeared everywhere,*
*like that plate full of ketchup, I was immersed in blood, I gagged*
*and passed out.*

No one tells you what it's like to heal from the physical pain of abortion, let alone the emotional pain that your mind-body-spirit never forgot. My first abortion was horrific, so you might be wondering why the heck I had a second one. Me too. As a teen I was vulnerable, naïve, stubborn (still am), and desperately wanted love. I wanted to be popular, to be noticed. Who doesn't, right? But being pregnant in my teens was not the kind of attention I was looking for. I was just looking for someone to love me. So clueless at 16, I made an adult decision to dive deep into this "love relationship" only to suffer more hurt and pain, which, by the way, I found normal because my friends were experiencing the same type of relationship. So when I became pregnant a second time, I'm guessing not too long after the first one, I quickly buried that painful event and moved on, or so I thought.

Not knowing the exact timeline of when I aborted two beautiful souls no longer is my focus. I no longer beat myself up for my horrific choices nor do I dole out perpetual punishment. I finally and fully understand that God forgives me, and I finally extended that forgiveness to yours truly. Recently, I was able to acknowledge that in God's eyes, I am pure, I am valued, I am loved. I no longer fret in my mind what life would have been like if I had chosen life for my babies. I was blessed with visions and dreams of them, where I saw them happy and content. A handsome son and beautiful daughter, he with dark hair, her with golden blonde. I realized at one point in my journey, my babies needed names. After much prayer, I decided to name my son Michael and my daughter Tamara. Recently I had asked them for forgiveness. It was a beautiful, sacred moment.

The healing journey has been long, I have learned that it is a daily journey and there is no magic pill, no instant fix, no one and done. It takes commitment, work, and time. Implementing the modalities I learned over the years has helped me tremendously to heal not only from these two painful events, but all that life has dealt me.

Brain dumps help me go deep to the root of my pain, dig it up, identify it, and process it fully. Is it hard? You bet! Did I want to quit? Absolutely! Did I drudge up painful memories? Yes! But I didn't give up, my stubborn self wanted healing, peace, and joy more than anything else. I was doing the work and at times it felt like I was spinning my wheels. Two steps forward, five steps back, counselor after counselor, group therapy, books on anger. I mean, how much counseling does a girl need before she gets better?

Healing is a journey, a daily choice to decide you want to take a new path, open a different door. My old self fought. It was easy to be angry, to have explosive moments, to blame others, to get drunk on a bottle of wine - drowning my sorrows or spending hours shopping for pretty items. I messed with cocaine. It did not numb the pain. I overate, I tried to claw my way out of the pit. The darkness smothered me. The pain was unbearable. With my Catholic upbringing, I knew I was damned to hell, damned to eternal punishment, never to be forgiven, but I begged God anyway. All of these thoughts were brought to the surface with my first brain dump. Was it scary? You bet. Was it hard? Absolutely. Did it help? 100%. I have been doing them ever since. Why? Because I was tired, exhausted. I was done with a temporary fix. My unhealthy coping mechanisms just put a band aid on the pain and I was so done with masking it. I was done with putting on my happy face, stuffing and exploding, pretending everything was alright.

Another modality I implemented is a painful event worksheet. I learned this when I took a 29-week class called The Healing Journey[3]. Truly understanding my pain, false beliefs and processing them head on, released a lot of hurt buried deep within my mind. These sheets have been a weekly practice for me and have been a wonderful tool of healing.

These days I practice brain dumps at least once a week. The brain dump has been one of the most important exercises that I've done to heal from my past hurts to forgive the girl inside. When I realized where my pain originated from, I was able to process the root cause of my anger and understand why I held onto unforgiveness. I know you might be scared, but don't let fear keep you in bondage. Your thoughts need to be processed. Get them out of your head so you can process your feelings.

As time goes on you will find that you look forward to the brain dump. These days I am in the habit of writing one word at the top of the page and writing all that comes to mind when I reflect on it. All I know, brain dumps are here to stay. They help tremendously. Okay. You might be scared, do it anyway. Don't let fear control you.

As a certified Oola Life Coach I walk my clients through seven blockers, one of them being fear. Did you know we are only born with two fears? The fear of falling and the fear of loud noises. All other fears are learned and can be unlearned. So, you need to unlearn your fear of writing something down because you are afraid someone is going to see it or you're afraid of what might come out. If someone sees it, so what? What's the worst thing that could happen?

Write it down and tuck in the drawer. Your brain will be prepared for it if it does happen. Don't be like me. I literally spent 30 years yelling and screaming at everybody because I never knew how to properly express myself. Then I would drown myself in wine and drink until I passed out just to numb the pain and start the cycle all over again. What unhealthy coping mechanisms are controlling you? Do the brain dump.

You know what else a brain dump will do for you? It will

allow you to stop hiding, stop putting on the "happy face." Oh boy did I wear it well. I hid behind all my volunteer duties. None of it helped with my pain. It didn't heal my hurts. All it did was distract me from the misery deeply rooted in my heart. Why choose to live that way when there's a better way? Why not heal from the inside out so you can live the life that you're meant to live? God put you on His earth for a purpose. He gives each of us unique gifts and talents that only you possess to use to glorify Him. Why not live your purpose? Why spend all day in misery? Friends, don't do what I did for over 30 years. Holding onto shame and guilt did nothing but keep me in bondage. I wasted time arguing with myself. You need to let go of self-sabotage. We cannot change our past, but we certainly can change how we respond to it.

My daily affirmation: God is my provider, my protector, my power. HE alone is who I trust and rely on when I deal with all that comes my way. When I continuously cried out to God, He provided the tools I needed to heal. Do I still have bouts of anxiety, anger, and arguments? Of course. But the way I respond is so much healthier than before this lifechanging strategy.

Ready to give it a try?

Let me walk you through it.

**Step one:** Grab a paper and pen. Are you ready to release all the negativity in your head?

**Step two**: Set your timer for 15 minutes and write. Write whatever comes to mind, and if you get stuck, write "I'm stuck" or "pity party." Write whatever, just don't let that pen leave the paper while the time is ticking. When you are done writing, set it aside. Drink a tall glass of water with lemon in it. You may feel exhausted when you are done. You may feel lighter. Listen to your body and take care of you. Tuck your notepad away, let your brain rest. Tomorrow you will complete step three. For now, just be.

**Step Three**: You must wait 24 hours before doing this. No cheating! Set your timer for 15 minutes. Start reading what you wrote and circle words or phrases that are repetitive. Categorize them and notice the patterns. Choose one category to work on. Write it on a separate sheet of paper. The rest, write diagonally across the paper: "I'm sorry, please forgive me, I forgive you, thank you, I love you." Now ask God for forgiveness. When you are truly remorseful, He forgives you and remembers your sin no more. Forgive yourself the way God forgives you.

I chose to forgive people who hurt me, but I never forgave myself for what I did until January 2019. That was a long time to hold onto unforgiveness, shame and guilt. When I think of my babies in Heaven, Michael and Tamara, I think of my horrific choices, and all the hurt I caused others because I hurt so badly. I know my healing journey isn't over. I know I am truly healed from my past and at the same time, I will never forget what I did or the events that happened. I do know I have a modality set in place that quickly redirects my negative outbursts and helps me focus on my true purpose rather than keeping stuck in that deep dark pit.

You see, I knew God wanted me to share my story to help women heal from this pain of unforgiveness, especially when it involves an unplanned pregnancy. But I was disobedient until August 2020. Why? Because I was petrified. Fear paralyzed me and kept me stuck. I wanted to blame my stubbornness but honestly, every time I uttered the word abortion I would break down in tears and deep bitterness would burn inside of me.

When I became a Certified Oola Life Coach, that's when I learned to conquer fear. Now I do things scared but most importantly I rely on my life verse: Proverbs 3:5: *Trust in the Lord with all thine heart; and lean not unto thine own understanding.* You see, when we refuse to forgive, refuse to process our hurts, we are declaring that we don't trust our Creator.

We are called to love one another. How can you love someone when you're too busy living in the past or depending on drugs and alcohol to get you through the day? These addictions distort our thought process, they are a distraction from freedom. How clear is your thought process when you're drowning in alcohol or high as a kite from the blunt you just smoked? Or maybe you have a "cleaner" addiction such as retail therapy or eating a sleeve or two of Oreo cookies in one sitting and you justify it because you are so sad, angry, and upset. You don't know what else to do and it feels good at the time. Then the next day you regret it because the pain is even worse. Stop the excuses and set the timer, then just write. Write whatever comes to mind. Don't question it. I practice this weekly. When I first started, I did it daily. Make this your goal. Every day for 30 days, do a brain dump, make it a commitment, and see how your heart begins to heal. I dare you.

I finally and fully
understand that God
forgives me, and I
finally extended that
forgiveness to yours truly

# Chapter Eight

## OVERCOMING GUILT

Guilt is one of the blockers that keep us stuck in fear. Myth buster: People cannot make you feel guilty. People cannot make you feel anything. You are the author of your own thoughts and feelings. Only you can make yourself feel guilty. Guilt is often self-made. After you have made a poor or horrific choice, a decision that was not optimal, that lacked a favorable outcome, or worse yet hurt others, it is really a challenge to overcome that guilt.

I know. I held onto shame and guilt until I was 51 years old. You see, my 16-year-old brain did not understand the long-term effect that two abortions would have on my psyche. Oh, if I only knew. Burying the pain made it worse. The angry monster that masked guilt overpowered my personality and I rightfully earned the label bitch. Proud to show my tough attitude, I went to great lengths to prove how strong I was. I was broken inside, like shattered glass strewn on the hard pavement. There was no hope, or so I thought.

It took me a long time to figure out the truth, to understand that there is grace and that I deserved it, even though I didn't believe it. What did I believe? That I was beyond forgiveness, that I did the unforgivable, and God was never going to forgive me, love me, nor would I ever be good enough. A million penances would not wipe out my crime - a murdered-at-large. To wipe away my shame, I spent a lot of time reading books about overcoming guilt and setting healthy boundaries. What do healthy boundaries have to do with overcoming guilt you ask? In my healing journey, I realized that I allowed people to make decisions for me. A people-pleaser at heart, I allowed others to take advantage of me.

My self-esteem was so low. I lacked confidence. Self-sabotage kept me chained to my past. I was so angry joy was blocked.

When I learned to set healthy boundaries and began to voice my concerns and desires, my attitude changed. I was less quick to have explosive outbursts. I realized that overcoming guilt was challenging. I could not do it on my own. Scripture helped. I prayed to Jesus for forgiveness and truly was sorry but (yes, there is always a but), I still felt guilty. Shame permeated my being. I could not escape it. Extending forgiveness to others was a walk in the park; however, to myself, not so much. I didn't deserve grace and spent hours in my head convincing my 20-year-old self, my 30-year-old self, my 40-year-old self, and my 50-year-old self that I did not deserve forgiveness nor would I ever be worthy of it.

Hours wasted in my head, beating myself up, asking the same question repeatedly, "Why? Why did I make that decision, not once but twice! Why?" That moved to the "If only" conversations in my head. "If only I would have known better if only I wasn't such a fool if only I could see the signals if only I had listened to my friends or my family…" Have you been there? Reflecting on that time in my life, I often wonder if it could have been prevented. Why did I lose my virginity at 16 years old, why didn't I take precautions? (That story is in my soon-to-be-published book, *Let's Get Real: Peaceful Resolutions to Chaotic Conversations*). Why did I allow this incident to happen? Could I have prevented it? My 50-year-old self thinks this should have never happened. But it did, and we all know we cannot change the past even though I so desperately wanted to. Guilty! It does not matter how I looked at my choice. Ultimately that's exactly what it was, my choice. I was not coerced into it, no one threatened me or held a gun to my head, or blackmailed me. I weighed my options and made my choice, not once but twice. And I swore after the second time, that if I became pregnant again prior to my marriage, I would be old enough to be a mom and I would choose life. And that is exactly what happened. At age 17 I became pregnant for the third time and had my beautiful son five months after my 18th birthday.

You may be wondering how I was so naïve (I really wanted to type stupid, but then it meant my father, who told me I was stupid for as long as I could remember would be right. Besides, it is such a harsh label). Some things are out of our control, others, not so much. For whatever reason, relationships in my teens were broken. I was sad, angry, depressed, and anxious. I just wanted to be loved, appreciated, liked, to fit in. Yes, I looked to others to raise my self-esteem, not realizing that it was Negative Nellie who kept me chained to my low self-worth. I did not know anything about positive affirmations or encouraging words, pep talks were not in my vocabulary (I didn't make the cheerleading squad in 7th grade, go figure), let alone give myself compliments. I often wonder why it took me so long to begin my healing journey. Now I know it is not one and done. It is called a journey because that's exactly what it is. It's a daily choice, a daily walk. Every day we are faced with right or wrong, left or right, yes or no. Nowadays, I carefully weigh my options, predicting the outcome to assure I will not feel guilty over my decisions.

What we think, we feel, and what we feel manifests our actions. Choose guilt, you will be guilty. Stinking thinking will keep you in the dark. It will keep you chained to your past, it will keep you stuck, and most importantly it will keep you unbalanced in all areas of your life. What are you guilty of? Are you holding onto it and letting it rule your life?

Perhaps your relationships are broken, you are feeling guilty that you're not bringing in income, you're relying on your spouse for support, or maybe you have turned to unhealthy coping mechanisms to mask the shame and guilt. Whatever you are struggling with, it is time to accept it. It's time to process it. It's time to begin your healing journey.

Here are three tips to overcome guilt:

*Tip 1*: Write down specifically what you feel guilty about.

*Tip 2*: Write across the offense "I'm sorry."

*Tip 3*: Seek forgiveness for yourself and anyone you may have offended. Tell God you're sorry and ask Him to forgive you and to set you free from the pain and hurt you have caused.

Acknowledging your guilt and processing the hurt it has caused is one of the keys to healing. Instead of beating yourself up or trying to punish the offender, embrace the event and learn from it. Feeling guilty is a normal response to things that offend us; ignoring it will keep you in bondage.

Are you ready to be set free?

.

Extending forgiveness to others was a walk in the park; however, to myself, not so much

# Chapter Nine

**POSITIVELY SPEAKING**

I would have described my 13-year-year-old self as snarky. I thought it was a good word for me. However, my peers thought "bitch" was even better and handed me a "License to Bitch" card. What an honor, said no one ever. My 52-year-old self shared that story in a conversation with a fellow life coach and she replied that being called a "bitch" was an honor as it stands for "Babe in Total Control of Herself." I was in control of myself, at least that's what I believed.

My anger controlled me. I would tell people off in a heartbeat. Constantly on guard for someone to offend me, my MO was to attack first. Yes, I always assumed my peers were against me. After all, I did not like myself so why would anyone else. My words spewed out like venom, screaming at the top of my lungs. My fits always triggered an asthma attack. Here I was 5 feet high, weighing 90 pounds, my facial expression twisted in anger, my body keeled over gasping for air. Real tough. How can someone full of rage be positive? My guidance counselor suggested a class on being assertive. She explained that my anger needed to be redirected. With the proper tools, I would learn to express myself with authority. I liked being in charge and hey, I would do anything to get out of study hall.

My new perspective made me realize that we all deserve respect. I finally understood that I was not the only one dealing with stuff. Everyone is. No one is perfect. You cannot judge a book by its cover. Everyone needs forgiveness. When we change our perspective, we change our thought process, which changes how we feel about things. As a result, you then have a new outcome, a peaceful conversation, no yelling, no screaming, no name-calling. Just an exchange of words that promotes peace.

Realizing that I could express myself "quietly" was a game-changer for my reputation. I slowly lost the BITCH title and learned to express myself with a controlled voice. It was nice not complaining all the time, and people-pleasing became a thing for me. I loved the positive feedback I received when I helped someone. Smiles were better than frowns, and I yearned for positivity in my life. I also learned to love challenges.

One of my biggest challenges was hiding the abortions from my mom. She was the last person I ever wanted to find out about my horrific act. It went against everything she taught me and believed in. I knew she would have been disappointed, angry, sad. There was no way I could tell her. I did not have to, someone else did. To my surprise, she had a positive reaction. We talked about it in a loving way. It was my sin, my burden, and she wished I would have come to her. Really? I assumed her response would be negative. In my 16 years of living with her, everything was negative, always yelling and screaming. Why on earth would she respond positively? It was weird. I never expected her to be supportive. I learned that in times of trouble, peaceful conversations resulted in peaceful resolutions.

Keeping calm when you are angry is a challenge. My immediate response is to snap so I had to learn to keep my cool by practicing positive reactions to negative outbursts. Acknowledging what the person said, reaffirming their words results in a better outcome. You might not always agree with what someone is saying, and maybe you are having a bad day yourself, but it is important to think positively. Remember, what you think determines how you feel, which determines how you act. This takes practice, but it is well worth it. Besides, how do you think the person with the negative outbursts responds? Positively of course! Are you scratching your head wondering what the heck I'm talking about? Ahh, the human mind.

See, when someone verbally throws upon you, spewing their anger, calling you names, threatening you, blaming you, your immediate response is to what? To do the same! Well, you have to try a new way. Who wants to waste all that time and energy fighting and spewing ugliness? So, the next time you verbally attacked, wherever you are, whoever you are with, try this:

Stay calm.
Look the person in the eye.
Confidently say: "I see you are upset; how can I help."

Do you know what that raging lunatic will do? They will get all flustered and garble their words! They didn't expect that response. You threw them for a loop. So what happens next? Of course, the angry fella will try to get you to react negatively. This is the important part. Stay CALM! Keep cool. Maintain healthy boundaries. How? Listen to what the person is saying. Understand it most likely has nothing to do with you. Acknowledge their hurt and you may even have to say you're sorry (don't overthink it, you may just be sorry you were in that place at that moment).

Instead of having a raging fit yourself, choose to have a peaceful conversation with a positive response. This takes A LOT of practice. Practicing daily gratitude, putting on the full armor of God (see Ephesians 6:11-18) will help you stay focused and in the right mindset. My relationships improved; my message was finally heard. There is a reason we have two ears and one mouth; listening is a skill. Hear what the other person is saying and extend the courtesy to hear them out. Forcing our beliefs on someone and insisting they see things our way invites pushback. We all have a choice. It is not our job to control the situation.

The next time your anger is triggered, and you feel the rage build up, ask yourself, "Why am I having a negative outburst? How can I turn this into a positive reaction?" Be aware of your triggers.

A lot of families deal with kids who blatantly refuse to do their chores. Rather than yell and scream at your child, layout the expectations beforehand, and dole out appropriate consequences if they do not keep their part of the bargain. When the family is part of the solution, the problem goes away. Weekly family meetings are golden. It takes care of the negative outbursts and everyone knows what is expected of them.

Positively speaking promotes peaceful conversations. I have practiced this repeatedly. Somedays I am more challenged than others. I do not like getting angry. It takes a lot of energy and then there is the make-up part. When I am successful in implementing my assertiveness training I learned way back in junior high, I am joy-filled and at peace. Why not give it a try?

# the power of affirmations

**SPEAK WORDS THAT EDIFY ENCOURAGE & ENLIGHTEN**

You cannot judge a book by its cover. Everyone needs forgiveness

# Chapter Ten

Ooh, la, la - the feeling you get when you wake up every day feeling fantastic! A life of less stress, more balance and greater purpose. A lifestyle that is all that and more is called the Oola Life. We want better connections with family and friends, better health and more vitality, more money at the end of the month, and financial security for our future. We want to go to a job that we love, we want to have fun in life, and we want to live a life filled with purpose. But most of us don't. We get swallowed up by the unbalanced world around us and find ourselves the opposite of an Oola Life. We find ourselves stressed, out of balance, and with little to no direction in life.

I found out about Oola in July 2020. My daily healing journey kept me on a quest to find balance. I knew something was wrong. My emotions were all over the place and even though the modality I had in place made a powerful impact on balancing my mood swings, I still fought the demons inside. I continuously prayed to God asking Him to show me the way, show me how to live for Him, how to do His will, His way, how to serve heart-to-heart. Then came Oola.

When I first implemented the framework, I was amazed at the impact it had on my mindset. I just had to become an Oola Certified Coach with Green Gap Certification. A missing piece in my healing journey, this modality propelled me to my final goal, paying off debt incurred due to insecurity and emotional spending – an unhealthy coping mechanism that chained me for almost 10 years. Yes, I had stinking thinking around money. You could say that was the nucleus of my emotional rollercoaster.

Focus. To put it in perspective, you can have all the tools you need to heal, but if you don't use them consistently, they are worthless. The Oola Life helps you focus on seven key areas. The 7 F's are:

*~Fitness ~Finance ~Family ~Field~Faith ~Friends ~Fun*

I love the concept of balance in these seven areas not only because I am partial to seven, but it really helped me keep things balanced. As you can see, these are the seven key areas of life. When you are balanced in all areas, life is joy-filled and well, balanced.

Before Oola, I was unbalanced and fighting for peace. Misery outweighed the joy-filled days despite my efforts to overcome it, especially when it came to my finances. I grew up poor, my family never vacationed, nor did we have a lot of money for extras, like more than two pairs of shoes. I had my first full-time job at the age of 11 when I babysat for the summer. The money was used to buy my school clothes. I did not think it bothered me until I went to junior high, where I was mocked for not dressing like the "rich" kids. A phrase I recall my mom repeating was, "Money goes where money is" and, "I have to borrow from Peter to pay Paul." Now, I was not sure who Peter and Paul were, but I understood the concept and always asked, "Why can't the money go where I am?" One of my favorite questions as a wee one was, "why"? I questioned everything and learned as much as I could. So of course, I started researching about money and why my family was so poor.

In my 20's I fell into trouble with credit cards. Dangerous and undisciplined, the "I-want-it-now mentality" was one of the unhealthy coping mechanisms I used to hide behind my shame and guilt. I justified my poor spending habits by convincing myself I needed the things to get ahead, to clothe my child, to get a better job - I had all the excuses. My self-sabotage ended up in my filing for bankruptcy at only age 22! This poor relationship resurfaced in my forties. You see, I wanted to fit in. I wanted to appear well-off and I didn't want my son to do without. What I didn't know when I opened my first credit card was the why. Why did I need material things to make me happy? Why did I need to charge an outfit a day to feel good about myself and my situation? I had a strong conviction that I didn't want my son to grow up poor like me. So I tried to overcompensate. It didn't work out too well. I made a promise to myself that day that I would never be in debt again.

I broke my own promise and quickly fell into debt in 2014. I diligently pursued plans, worked overtime, picked up a side gig, and even cut up credit cards. Talk about regressing into misery. Every payday I would get sick to my stomach. I would tell myself, "I will get out of this. I will just follow these easy steps". The only thing I escaped was balance. The debt took hold of me and the more I tried to pay it off, the more I failed. Why was I such a mess?

Oola was the answer. Implementing the principles of the Green Gap strategy (email me to learn more at lisadthe-facetscoach@gmail.com) helped me create S.M.A.R.T goals, a concept adopted from George Doran in 1981 who came up with SMART goals. He suggested that each written goal follow this S.M.A.R.T format:

This helped me improve my relationship with money. I also incorporated another technique which I share in the next chapter. In my research, I realized that change occurs when things are in alignment. The first step is to have the right mindset. You need to establish SMART goals and then write them down. Failure to write equals failure to succeed. Writing seals the deal.

This was one of the best tools to implement in my healing journey. When I realized that my financial crisis was because of my emotional rollercoaster, my desire was to have control (when I was out of control). I was able to break free from this unhealthy coping mechanism. Seeing the written goals helped me to navigate my negative thoughts and false beliefs I had around money.

The reason I could not succeed before was because it was an addiction. I was addicted to "gambling", to 0% credit cards. My challenge was to pay them off before their interest rate expired, which I succeeded to do for many years until it became exhausting.

Caught up in my thoughts, not sure how to navigate things, hiding it from my family, I kept the cycle spinning until I crashed. With no sense of direction that is what happens, you crash. Spending time trying to figure it out in my head resulted in an increase in my anxiety. Back to ground zero. I wanted out. I needed to cut the bitter root of debt from my past. I started to dig deep and finally uncovered the secret to my bondage. The deep hurt and bitter roots of shame and guilt from my teen years were buried in my subconscious, revealing lies that weaved false beliefs into my inner psyche around money and value - the value of myself and who I truly was. Because I focused on being poor and "money going where money was," I believed that the only way I could have money was to "borrow it from Peter to pay Paul." Enlightening! By accepting this as a lie and affirming the truth, I was able to discover the true meaning of financial blessings.

At a crossroad, I had two choices - to trust in the Green Gap method or continue doing it my way. (Despite other financial courses I took, the missing link for me was the accountability I had with a coach, which is one of the reasons I became a life coach). Embracing the fact that retail therapy was an addiction for me, accepting that I used 0% credit cards as a crutch, and knowing I was not alone, was the catapult to freedom. Write it down! This is something so simple yet so effective especially when it comes to finances. The concept of telling your money where to go versus it telling you, helped me balance not only my finances but the other areas as well.

If you're on an emotional rollercoaster with finances or any of the other F's, it's time to be balanced. It may seem overwhelming at first, but chunk it down, take baby steps, and watch your Oola Life unfold. When you map it out, you design the blueprint, the personalized plan specific to you so you can achieve your goals and dreams. It begins with a self-assessment. Determining where you are on the Oolawheel is the beginning of your roadmap. To learn more about this, visit https://www.oolalife.com/step1. Embracing this concept was the final key to my healing journey. If you are overwhelmed and stuck, tired of riding the emotional rollercoaster, it's time to grab your blueprint. Work with a coach, set your S.M.A.R.T goals, and move into a balanced life so you can live your purpose.

Did you know you are designed by God for greatness and a purpose? When you are living an attitude of gratitude, you are following the blueprint of the 7 F's. You are able to move forward in all areas of your life, including forgiveness. Whatever your addiction, it is time to break free and begin your healing journey. Release the negative mindset. Accept your past hurts, broken promises, those that you hurt or hurt you. Embrace shame and guilt and remove the blockers that keep you stuck. Ditch false beliefs. Learn from your past and look for the treasure amongst the trials. Your experience is real. It does not define you. It is not who you are. It's where you've been and there is a valuable lesson to be taken from each hurt, each shameful event, each ounce of guilt. Grab your pen and paper, write down your S.M.A.R.T goals, and watch your shame, guilt, unforgiveness, worry, and strongholds lift.

Forgiveness is a choice, and that choice begins with you. It begins with you seeing beyond your offenses. When you do, and you embrace the modality, feel the boulder lift from your shoulders. For the first time in decades, I was truly living a joy-filled, fun, and balanced life. Ready to master your S.M.A.R.T. goals?

Forgiveness is a choice
and that choice
begins with you.

# Chapter Eleven

What just happened? As I stood on my deck on that hot summer night, I was bewildered and fascinated. For the first time in my life, I felt a burden lift from my shoulder. That is how I felt the first time I did an aroma freedom reset. It literally took five minutes. I knew I had to learn more. When I signed up for Nora's free group, I had no idea what I was getting into. I just knew I was eager to learn how to turn my side gig into a profitable source of income so I could sponsor women through CompassCare. My dream is to sponsor 30 women each month who are facing unplanned pregnancy so they can choose life. I joined this challenge in hopes to learn how to grow an online business centered around Young Living products. Eager to turn my side gig into a service to others, I went with the flow of this live event on Facebook.

So here I was, following along the guided breathing session to find myself within minutes releasing a repressed emotion, one that haunted me for years. I had no idea what this process was, but I knew I needed it in my life. The simple steps created by Dr. Benjamin Perkus, a Clinical Psychologist who incorporated breathwork, accompanied with Young Living Essential oils' memory release blend - Frankincense, Lavender, and Stress Away - broke an emotional chain I never thought possible.

The first step to the reset was to think of a current overwhelming or negative situation, followed by a reflection of negative thoughts that accompany it. You then recognize the emotion. You must choose a one-word feeling that describes the situation. This is followed by identifying where in your body you feel the negativity.

The next step is to close your eyes and think back to a time when you felt this same way. Once you have the memory, you place equal drops of each oil in the palm of your hand. Rubbing your hands together, you make a scent tent (cupping your hands around your nose) and breathe in the memory release blend, inhaling deeply through the nose. As you do this, you reflect on the circumstance, the memory, the negative words, and the one-word feeling. The smell immediately hits your olfactory system and boom! After a few breaths, your whole being relaxes.

I will always remember how I felt the first time I did aroma freedom - like a brand new woman. I simply had to learn more. I could not help but want to dig deeper. If I could release a stuck emotion with an aroma reset, just think of the breakthrough with a full session. I dove into a three-day challenge and from there, I signed up to be certified. This practice has helped thousands heal from past hurts, release negativity, break free of addictions, and achieve goals thought to be impossible.

Who knew that just breathing in this memory release blend and implementing specific steps could make such a difference? I don't understand how I missed this technique in all my years of counseling. The first time I practiced Aroma Freedom was in May 2020; I have since incorporated it as a daily practice. A quick reset helps me to balance my emotional rollercoaster. Just think of all the time I could have saved had I known about this when it was first introduced. At one point in counseling, I learned to count to 0 and take deep breaths. I do not recall when I started the practice, sometime in my early 40s. I do remember that I kept forgetting to incorporate it as a modality. When I did remember, it was well after my explosive outburst. I was instructed to be on the lookout for anger erupting. Being aware of your body signals is important to ward off explosive behavior. For me, it started with butterflies in my stomach. As soon as I felt it, I was supposed to stop, start counting to 10 while taking deep breaths through the nose and slowly releasing it through my mouth, keeping in the rhythm of 10. It worked when I remembered to do it, however not as quickly as the Aroma Freedom. With Aroma Freedom, it was immediate. In such a short time, I watched the brick wall I had built so high around me completely crumble. Talk about sealing in true forgiveness. My brick wall is now a beautiful garden fence, 3 feet high and surrounded with sunflowers and benches where you can sit and read or just be. Aroma Freedom has been a huge part of my healing journey. Even when I recall hurtful memories, I am able to safely process it knowing when I allow the memory to ebb and flow, acknowledge and process the emotion, I will truly be free. When I can go back and recall a hurtful event and process it, I am replacing the unforgiveness with forgiveness. If you have not tried this, I strongly urge you to book a session with me. I will give you the first one complimentary, just mention that you read it here and email me at lisadthefacetscoach@gmail.com to schedule a time. It will be the best thing you will ever do to help balance your emotions.

F: Faith

E: Expands in

A: Abundance when you

R: Release fear

Here's what some of my clients say:

***S. Mitchell 1/23/21:*** *For me what was amazing about Lisa is how comfortable she makes you feel and talking you through the process. I went to a place visually that I had never even been before and had no clue I could even go to that place. I'm writing this several hours after, and it amazes me how I feel and how reflective I am of* *the process. Lisa makes you feel safe to go deep. Look forward to my next session to see what else I learn about myself. Thank you, Lisa.*

\*\*\*\*

*J. **Gordon** 1/11/21: She is very helpful at helping me be more specific with my goals. Also very supportive and positive which allowed me to feel comfortable.*

\*\*\*

*C. **Shay** 2/1/21: Thank you so much for our 1:1 AFT today. Was remarkable, the change from hate to calm! So gracious of you!*

\*\*\*

*J. **Wenzel** 9/2020: I truly enjoyed my aroma therapy release session w/ Lisa. I went into the appt w/ some things on my mind & an intention to focus on forgiveness, I felt my inability to clear my head up was holding me back from moving forward to my best self. I could tell Lisa was so passionate & a calming force. She made me feel comfortable during the session to get vulnerable which isn't something most of us are probably used to doing but we want the connection needed to make the shift. She was non judgmental, calm and gave me great insight as she guided me through the session. I felt an pretty immediate release and it set the tone for where I'm headed. Just book an apt you won't regret it!*

When I can go back
and recall a hurtful
event and process it,
I am replacing the
unforgiveness with
forgiveness

# Chapter Twelve

**A BLISSFUL
ENDING**

The first time I shared my story I was petrified. It was in October 2020. I did it scared. I almost canceled the event I chose to share it in. A tap on my shoulder, a still small voice, said "just do it." Desperate for peace, I practiced my brain dump exercise and Aroma Freedom. I applied my Oola training to get through the fear blocker. I will always picture myself very clearly the first day I shared it publicly. I was sitting in my home office, feet curled up on my black desk chair. The sun was shining bright that Tuesday afternoon. I was on my weekly group coaching call. I was in the hot seat inquiring about my niche. I remember my coach told me to stop self-sabotaging myself. Wake-up call.

As a certified Oola LifeCoach, I knew that fear was a blocker, I knew it was keeping me from sharing my deepest, darkest secret. The pain was so fresh, I was embarrassed and filled with shame and guilt. It took me 36 years to forgive myself now I had to share it with others. I knew God was calling me in service to help other women stuck in shame and guilt. So many face unplanned pregnancies and due to false beliefs and lies, they conclude that abortion is the only answer. Friends, it is NOT the only answer. The life that grows inside of you is a blessing - it's God's divine timing, a miracle to be treasured and loved and valued. I stayed in prison for over three decades realizing my crime was against God, realizing my choices kept me chained to the deep hurt and pain I felt every time I tried to ignore the root cause. I remember the day I chose to forgive myself. Although I spent years extending forgiveness, I never offered it to myself. Self-sabotage kept me stuck in fear.

Then one day, a cold wintry day in January 2019, as I sat in the chair of the Healing Journey class, I chose to forgive yours truly. I will never forget that day. When I said the words out loud: "Lisa, please forgive me,"[4] I immediately felt 100 pounds lighter. It was like a boulder was lifted from my body. The fear, the stubbornness, the shame, the guilt, the self-sabotage - gone! I thought that was the final step. Never in a million years did I know that God wanted me to share my story with others. It was one thing to forgive myself but a whole new ballgame to share it with others. I knew I had to do it, and I had to do it scared. In Oola we have a formula, "Ready, Set, Go." Applying this principle got me through the fear.

I will never forget what I did. It will always be a pain point. I have found the more I share, the less it hurts. I feel comforted knowing that I am helping someone in the same position. Instead of focusing on the negativity and referring to myself as a murderer, I reflect on how it shaped my life, how it shaped my motherhood, how it shaped my thoughts, and most importantly, how I see others. I learned that we all mess up. We all have skeletons in our closets, past choices we have made that we are not proud of, choices that we hide behind in hopes no one will find out. Some we choose to stay hidden, to turn to unhealthy coping mechanisms, to allow the fear, shame, and guilt to keep us in that deep dark pit. Some choose to hold on tight to unforgiveness, refusing to believe that freedom is in forgiveness.

It is a choice, a daily choice, a daily healing journey. I have learned to love unconditionally and to respect people for who they are not what they have done. Our past choices do not define us. I learned a long time ago that sin does not define us, it's not who we are. Love the sinner, hate the sin. We live in an unbalanced world, not one of us is free from sin. Can you imagine if we all walked around with a sign on our chest that displayed our sin? How different we would all see one another. Remember, where you are is not who you are. Your past choices do not define you, they shape you and you learn from your traumas. Instead of being a victim, turn your traumas into treasurers and be victorious.

I do not know where you're at - whether you are on a healing journey or stuck in your past, letting it paralyze you in fear. This, my friend, is an incredible modality, one that brought balance to my chaotic life. Before I began my healing journey, my life was a facade. On the outside, I looked all put together. The mask I wore hid so much. My heart was so heavy, laden with poison that I fed myself every day. I was overwhelmed, overweight, depressed, anxious, and turned to unhealthy coping mechanisms to get through the day. I struggled to meet simple goals, drowning in debt and sleepless nights. I was completely out of balance. It's a healing journey because that is exactly what it is, a journey, a step-by-step walk, a day-to-day choice. It all started with an attitude of gratitude. Being grateful changes your heart. It was the first step in knocking down my 6' x 6' x 6' white brick wall.

Incorporating Aroma Freedom and the S.M.A.R.T. goals created the balance I so desperately needed to stabilize my emotional rollercoaster. I realized one size does not fit all. Grasping for change led me to where I am today. Discovering the root of the problem, digging out the bitter root of shame and guilt, made room for healing. It was a choice, a journey, a modality that I wish I would have known when I first made my decision to abort two beautiful lives. When I accepted my horrific act and acknowledged my sin and hurt and pain, then I was able to begin my healing journey. Burying it does not get you anywhere. That is why you are stuck.

There is one way out. It is time to remove the blockers. Ultimately, it is your choice. Are you determined to be free or do you want to stay in that deep, dark pit? Ask yourself, "What is the worst thing that will happen if you decide to move through the shame, the guilt, the fear, and the unknown?" Ask yourself, "What is the best thing that will happen when you move past the blocker?" Think about this, how is it affecting your life now? What is keeping you from achieving your goal? Why is it controlling your thoughts? At the end of the day, what you think determines how you act and feel?

Triggers create chaos. Do you know what sets you off in a frenzy? Maybe fear paralyzes you, keeps your feet cemented to the floor or your lips sealed, burying your words to save yourself another argument. Unprocessed feelings do not go away. They manifest themselves as physical pain (see Chapter Two). Burying your feelings creates a pattern of repetition. You have two choices - either continue doing it your way or open a different door. Discover the secret to healing from the inside out. My life will never be the same. I know in my heart that God uses our experiences to help others. I know I was created for such a time as this. Again, I say God designed you for a purpose. Instead of burying yourself in your pain, why not uncover it and heal from it. Begin to peel back the layers, knock down the brick wall, open the door to your cage. However you see yourself - in a prison cell or a padded room - there is a way out. There is a different door. The choice is yours.

If you are ready to hold the keys to living a balanced life, I will share the strategy with you. I have a 12-week coaching program that helps women entrepreneurs, coaches, and team leaders surrender self-sabotage that keeps them stuck in fear so they can secure their soulmate clients, provide life-changing results, and 10x their income. It helps women release anger, frustration, & reliance on unhealthy coping mechanisms so they can live with balance, joy, freedom, fun & deep forgiveness for past choices. This program works because we focus on changing thoughts and patterns, setting goals, and implementing a unique strategic plan to change habits that improve your mind, body, and spirit. This unique modality is different from anything else you tried because it is tailored to you - no more one plan fits all.

We begin with a personal assessment which is the framework we use to customize the plan for your specific needs. Everybody is different so each plan is uniquely tailored to fit your needs to help you find balance in the areas you need it most.

Email me at lisadthefacetscoach@gmail.com for a free consultation to see if this program is right for you.

Are you tired of trying programs that are "guaranteed to get you results..." and within a week you go back to your old habits or worse set you don't see a change. Here are three reasons why my program is different from all the other programs you've heard about.

#1: Surrender self-sabotage & release fear. Transform effort into results, stay focused, and on track with daily accountability. By taking responsibility for the outcomes of your actions and decisions you will be successful in your personal transformation. Within the first 3 weeks, you will see significant changes in your daily habits, feel your emotions become more stable, and your mindset shift.

#2: Implementing S.M.A.R.T. goals is the key to consistency. During the weekly coach calls, we review your personal goals and assure you are on track for success. Adding my secret sauce to your daily routine gives you the mindset to break bad habits and stay focused on the end result you desire. Whether your goal is to gain self-confidence, rewire your mindset to attract clients, increase energy levels, or balance emotions consistently applying this key to your daily practices will get the results you desire.

#3: My custom-designed blueprint is tailored specifically to you making it the perfect strategy to achieve the results you desire. Think of your mindset as a wheel, when it is out of balance, it doesn't roll very well. Focusing on key areas, we pinpoint where the wobble is and focus on the ones that need the most attention. This proven strategy has helped hundreds of life coaches and team leaders improve and keep all areas balanced.

Results propel when we focus on accountability, consistency, and a strategic plan customized to your personal and professional life. Instead of wasting time on a yo-yo, one-size fit guide, get a strategic, customized plan tailored to your specific needs, and get the results you desire that will last a life-time when implemented daily. Surrender self-sabotage, release fear and implement healthy coping mechanisms so you can authentically and confidently provide life-changing results and create balance, freedom, and fun to catapult success for both you and your client.

Are you ready to surrender self-sabotage?
Are you ready to release fear?
Are you ready to forgive yours truly?
Ready? Set. Go! Let's do this!

# I learned that forgiveness is a choice.

# References

1. ^    www.southwestspineandpain.com/blog/physical-pain-
   sync-emotional-pain
2. ^       https://thefreedomsproject.com/item/400-80s-book-highlights-the-horror-of-abortion
3. ^ https://www.hishealinglight.org/healing-journey
4. ^ lisa a drennon, "Healing Journey" lisa drennon (lisa drennon, January 16, 2019).

Freedom Through Gratitude

https://lisadrennon.com/landing/three-dy-challenge-attitude-of-gratitude

CPSIA information can be obtained
at www.ICGtesting.com
Printed in the USA
LVHW070918200221
679499LV00025B/211